Entries

ISBN: **978-0-9791463-8-1**

Dedicated with love to
Jaime, Jono, Jason, Jen & Josh.

All proceeds from the sale of this collection of poems
will go directly to The Harry Chapin Foundation

ACKNOWLEDGEMENTS

I have been living with these poems for many years, putting them aside for family and other projects; many of them around Harry's music. I am grateful to the encouragement of family and friends who urged me to continue: to Maxine Green, my literary light and mentor; also, to Julie Fleck. Many thanks to the poetry group – Estha Weiner, Lisa Fleck, Kathleen Cochran, Phyllis Gutman, Ruth Handel, Judy Ryan, Mary Jane Mott. And thank you to Pegge Strella and my son, Josh, for helping to push this through to print and get another project to the finish line.

CONTENTS

Foreword   *i*

I   Tunneling Through

First Love   1
Homing In   2
Over Seas   5
Landscape   6
Melody   7
Chameleon   8
Puzzle   9
Contest   10
The Way Things Connect   11
A Current Carries Me   12
Treasure   13
Let Me Confess   14
Friend   15
Celebration   16

II   Time Outside Eden

Off Season   19
Tick Tock   21
Full House   23
Furniture   24
The Night Donkey   25
Out of Adam's Rib   27
Divorce   29
Woman   31
In Season   32
Perspective   34

III Separations

Birds of a Feather 37

Testing I 38

Deaf Mute 39

Dance 40

The Argument 42

Portrait 43

Separation at the corner of Santa Monica
    and La Cienega 44

Home Movies 46

Letter to Home 47

Nobility 49

Narcissus 50

Dinner for Two 51

Ambushed 53

IV Rituals

From Long Island to Bequia Bay 57

Because of You 60

Detoxification 62

Rain 63

Off Shore 64

Storm Warning 66

Contract 67

Equinox 69

V Beginning at the Dead End

First Step   73
Rescue   74
Parallels   75
Tapestry   77
Vibration   78
Stripping In   80
Imagine Moments of Soft Wonder   82
Circle   85

Notes on the Author   88

Dear Sandy,

By a heck, I did my homework - and I'm happy to say that you
in my opinion you have many excellent lines.

But the problem of offering advice is doubly embarrassing in my
case. For style is so personal a matter, one hesitates to neb; and even
Denis Donoghue, who has been generous to me, only credits me with but
several estimable poems.

But your rhymed verse (in "Imagine Moments of Soft Wonder") gave me
exactly what I need, to justify my "nebbing."

The situation as I saw it was this: Your free verse lines are too,
we might say, "diaristic." They make for a reader's "nebbing" in a quite
different sense. In your "Parallels" piece (with its epigraph from Anais
Nin), though it is but half-free, half-rhymed, an your ending states your
free-verse ideal:

> To chart the new.
> No scheme so great
> As to see tenderly,
> Straight into me, into you.

But no readers aren't seeing into either of you. They're being
invited to look at you when involved in doing situations as private as
sitting on the can.

I think that you need more distance in presenting the way of telling
your story. And your last poem, "Imagine," itself shows how your own
way of writing can provide it.

I think you might at least experiment with a few cases. For instance,
you you might try writing rhymed versions of "Melody," "Adam's Rib," and
perhaps "Birds of a Feather." (After all, no less a poet than Racine
began with a prose scenario which he "translated" into his alexandrines.)

I have mentioned poems which are closer to such experimental
presentation already. And my "scheme" would be the thought that, having
done the job with those, you'd see ways of transforming things now said,
plus finding grounds to omit others purely because they resisted such
formalization.

Why not give it a try? You have a lot of good stuff in there, and
tests of greater formalization might make more effective as a poem what
gets lost in the cause of sheer diaristic honesty. (I confess to now my-
self writing what I explicitly call "diarisms." But they involve a dif-
ferent order of purel formal twists.) Best luck, K. B.

i

FOREWORD

In 1922, Kenneth Burke used a Dial Press award to purchase 140 acres in Andover, N.J. with a lake and a number of houses. It became the weekend and summer home of the Burkes and Chapins and I spent several summers there. To most of the family, K.B. was just a father or grandfather, but I used to treasure sometimes driving him to engagements, staying with his wife, Libby, when he was travelling or just sitting at the breakfast table hearing about his early years in the Village and teaching at the University of Chicago and at Bennington. Occasionally, I could show him my poems. He wrote the letter at left in July, 1983.

S.C.

I Tunneling Through

First Love

I needed something to hang on to
as a swing ties to a tree;
a singular oak leaning into wind
over waves, all green.

What surprises, when you appeared
grounded, fearless of lightning,
capable of great journeys
within your asymmetry.

This rustling incessantly at the leaves,
sassy pitch and irreverence
struck a chord in me. It was the tree
that orchestrated the wind.

Even the night's closed eyes
could not simulate frailty under rough bark
and there was no moss.
All around my arms clutched brilliance.

It is difficult to feel compassion
for giants. Yet, I wanted to smooth
scars from an axe blow, to still
the agitation in the split trunk,

in order to affix my swing.

Homing In

The day after I lose my way,
homing pigeons invade
my ears, humming me dizzy,
reel off into smoke.

Convinced one bird will carry
a map, I rent a garret
with a dovecote,
press my eye to the grille.

There, I strain along rows
of headstones, sunburned
reflections of skyscrapers, scan
the horizon for their return.

I lock the door, shun neighbors.
Even opening the oven door evokes
a dungeon, where I tunnel through,
surface to find the street sign blank.

I set up my easel
by northern light, squeeze
dabs of color on the palette,
splash jolts of white,

then combinations of ochre,
blue, purple and gray,
blend each dusty spot
smooth and opaque.

I paint a covey of pigeons,
hear their bold clambering.
My knife gashes a torrent
of gray over angry scolding.

Next day I advertize
for a model. You come
with your guitar. You play
past the appointed hour,

snap up the blinds
to expose this castaway,
pull the bolt on all the locks
when I decide to pay.

I paint on the same
canvas, strong strokes
of yellow and white, the cover
peels to answer your song.

My palette knife dances
in rhythm to your guitar.
Clouds cease to cover and
I clear color under color,

dance deft arabesques
of flight and V formations,
a flock of wild geese
veers off the upper left.

A white swan wavers midair,
flutters on bare linen,
blur of violet
sprouts filigree of feathers.

I lay down my knife.
Only a fine brush will do
to lift the head, smooth the
spread wings close for landing.

Your fingers cease picking;
they slide and caress strings
while my brush untucks dove feet
that grip the edge, and rest.

I hold my breath until
just at the corner
the gold leg band
spells your name.

Over Seas

Over seas I surge on wave crests,
diffuse light on fast currents, compel
maneuvers, at once tactical and evasive,
above the undulating swell.

You appear so interested,
I pull out the throttle and go full steam
ahead. Then it is not the motor that matters,
but to set my course on your beam.

Suddenly, I am willing to abandon ship,
to dive into the deep, and surface near
enough to touch the light behind
your eyes, that try so hard to hear.

Landscape

I feel as though the shape of me
will naturally fold into you.
My mounds are your hollows.
Hills roll around valleys. New
layers heat crests
to flow into molten quiet.
Here is a landscape without
bones; no knuckles or elbows riot
on edge. Ridges meet and slide into right places.
None are walls. Embraces uncover
linings, crave combining. To be one.

Melody

He is playing his tune,
suggestive, promising more.
She matches in counterpoint,
testing, to find the tempo,
to search out the theme.
In concert, they interweave
his past and hers.

Notes climb stairways,
outside the bars.
The next step is hers.
She strikes boldly, scores allegro.
He urges his guitar,
alters the strum, doubles the chords.

She sings the harmony,
then abruptly adds
a variation, more melody.
He tosses phrases, strands.
The music escapes the page
but falls into an electrifying
cacophony to disguise
what was important.

The cadence flows andante,
to keep the music from ending.
She writes a chorus.
Now the music is words,
the strings caress.
Eyes meet in one voice,
rhythm living past
the song's end. I can't remember
who plays the last note.

Chameleon

My eyes are green, skin
translucent. My tongue
darts in perpetual motion
to fill spaces, to scale coarseness.
I slither, match surroundings,
watching. Waiting to be watched.
Sighted, I freeze, then bound,
just short of losing my tail.

I warm in slow light, resolve
and change colors. Trace
bright rays in brief flashes,
cracks of sun through a shutter.
Iridescent limbs blind invaders.
Poised over the trap door, alone,
I face in and out,
at once.

Puzzle

The question lingered
restless and
demanded. So
I answered, "No!"
It could have
pranced along
beside me or ahead
to test and play
with time and soon,
or late, answer itself.

Contest

You are Zeus, ambrosial
locks cascade down. Your
immortal head nods and
shakes great Mount Olympus.

Your thighs ripple
and sway. Marble calves
plant history
astride my side.

Arrogant sculpture from Mycenae,
you see me prone,
not yet flattened, but
flattered to be considered a foe.

I move closer, over
Mediterranean waves and
imagine Nefertiti
summoning slaves.

You, who dismiss and
diminish queens,
lower your powers,
full and armed.

I cross the Corinth,
scale Pelopennesian ground,
climb the Acropolis. Then,
I am Hera with crown.

The Way Things Connect

is by tight closings,
safety pins and snaps,
or by loosening, lifting
weight to air, opening wings
to desire outside us
because it's there.

The way things connect
is by gold bands
and silver chains,
or by invisible
fastenings.
Believe they are there!

A Current Carries Me

as I smooth beds and dry dishes,
gnaws at the back of my throat.
I fix a cup of tea. Then it curls
into my ribs and lower back.
I'm sure it's hunger.
Soon, as I grab an English muffin,
it moves on, circumventing
my pelvis, raising hair on my
belly, rests like a soft vacuum
blower in a hollow between my
thighs. Now I am under,
swept away to you.

Treasure

Champagne, long johns, notes on
windshields and glasses. Airborne
images are snowflakes melting
thru reason and disguise to adorn
shadows. Engraved on a word,
a touch, your eyes light. How wide,
how quiet, the moments
when our minds collide.
I will keep these treasures safe,
all the heart's stores,
wrapped in bright tissue colors,
every sweet thing, to be yours.

Let Me Confess

Bodies are not supposed to matter.
    They say it is not what's on the
    outside that counts.
    Looks are not important.

Then why is it I look for yours?
    Why is it I imagine it under others' clothes?
    Why is it I invest in it in absentia?
    Why is it I never lose the feel of it:
        the hard shape,
        the weight,
        the definitive mounds,
        the power of the thighs?

Anatomy is significant!
I will never be satisfied otherwise.

Friend

You, my trusted friend, were
the first day and the next,
a shield and then a key
to turn me loose.
When I lay dark, a ghost,
you watched just out of sight.
No word, no flame, but held
a host to time, a candle
in the wings for me to light.

Anticipating storms,
you soon divined
a lightning rod to catch
the strike and jolt.
You leashed the blinding flash
and held the stores,
offered radiant gifts,
one after one,
to pace each step of mine.

One of these days,
when I risk all again,
when waiting's through,
I'll meet some other friend,
and peel these careful clothes,
move to flesh and want.
Then you must know,
I know it can't,
But should be you.

Celebration

Now embraces open all
windows and doors! We throw
confetti over children first,
then the grownups. Streets sing,
neighbors hold hands, merchants
blow bold kisses. Even traffic
slows to wave and cheer at green
lights; pedestrians delay at crossings
to touch us. Everyone is lined up
to catch our bouquets.

II Time Outside Eden

Off Season

Snow drifts against the door,
wind chafes at the chimney,
keeping us in.
We, who are used to racing
last minute trains
and curtains calls,
drift inside our skin.

Now you strum a new song
and tap dance
with your visitors,
the Panasonic transistor
and the 11 o'clock
TV basket-
ball scores.

I juggle bits and pieces,
weak tea, a damp log on the fire,
peacock plume,
fuzz of dust on the brass
candle stand, a lost line
in my head, fidgetings that fuse
in a huge divider across the room.

The fire shrivels to a low, blue glow.
I could poke it,
let it die in the dark,
sweep ashes...
You leave
it all up to me
to make sparks.

Suppose I throw on one more log,
shed this too warm robe
and say it's June,
lie down at your feet,
spread out to sun
myself in firelight.
Will you play an old tune?

Tick Tock

For the third time tonight
the old kitchen clock bolts me upright;
motor rattles past
the speed limit, gasps
for breath. A bad case of the jitters,
I suspect, probably contagious.
Even flies are disgusted and brain
themselves against windowpanes.

I have been playing hide-and-seek
with particulars, wear sleep
for a blindfold. The minute
hand's manic chorus, "Still got to get it
all done,
all done,
all done," exaggerates my shame.
I pull the plug to short circuit the game,

turn on the light,
wipe windows, sweep dust, right
overturned chairs, line up
forks in tune with the spoons.
It's my move. I put in the plug,
count sixty seconds to a minute,
swallow the bait,
position shakers. My mate

and I cut a sturdy
team until the clock absurdly
yawns down to half-time.
Eyelids are not enough to cover
this long rehearsal.
I fix the clock, pretend
I'm ahead. Outside, a fluorescent moon
blinks my fortune.

The kitchen is overgrown
from the heavy scent of ozone.
I blow off bubbles
one by one,
reset the knob
to get even
and conceal my crime.
By morning the clock is back on time.

Full House

Your songs are full of clues,
there are two parts to me,
called Jenny and the one you use.
She was free and brought loving,
from older and experienced men,
slipped into your room, bare,
sat astride you tossing her hair
and breasts, riding away avarice
until light burned out the fear
in your chest. She fled
without even asking for a kiss.
Should I envy an old lost love
and one now dead of a tumor,
Why do you say to me, "I've got to find her?"

Now you bang through the broken door
across the boys' boots and books,
past Jenny's crib, into my night.
Without turning on the light
you undress, all meat hooks
and a clatter of stone chimes
around my ears, slip under the sheet
nudge my back until I meet
you and cover your bare chest
lightly with whispers.

Furniture

I am shopping for second-hand
furniture. Something's missing
from the perfect antiques and
fully restored. I need more
than a period and style,
more than a motif.

"Have buyer for family home and contents.
You may have dog."
Snapshots, high school yearbook,
packets of old love letters,
tattered doll, lovingly stored
for my someday-little-girl,
the antique wedding gown, assorted
paraphernalia, now the stranger's.

So, I, stripped of my past,
paw through others' dust
and refuse, seeking to restore my self.

The Night Donkey

Again, the night donkey romps,
the same one that rode my back
some weeks ago,
to stomp prints
of all the old negatives
that won't dissolve.

Who would have thought
a track for fat donkeys
runs on my back.
Syncopated beating
blacks out the winning; all the
numbers relate to the last race.

Paper clips hitch the lists,
check off the old score.
The racing sheet matches.
I flip the pack and
pick up the same names and
handicaps. There's no finish.

The donkeys increase in number:
I call it a rampage.
I'm not a cowboy.
I count heads, thumps,
and their reverberations.
Counting hurts.

They slow, slurp, blap,
plod in mud,
my vertebrae are redone in dung,
gum coats my back and calcifies.
In the morning,
the cast cracks.

Out of Adam's Rib

Legend has it,
the least of his
stout skeleton
fashioned her.

Shoulder, hip, pelvis,
skull or breast? No, from one
of many thin, bent bones
would woman occur.

Second fiddle! Afterthought!
No original and separate
sprout from
her-own inspired seed!

Just foster-fathered
replant, refinished
reproduction, this
redundant breed.

Little wonder that the
myth perpetuated
by Paul and the Papacy
confuses the fall.

On the one hand,
squired benevolent birth,
indentured maid,
 and chattel doll;

on the other, cast out
sinner, superfluous stuff,
for two thousand years,
unclean, undone.

Makes us long to lean
on something tough,
at the very moment we snap
the bone and run.

Divorce

With only one bit of advice,
"Don't drink the water,"
I fly alone,
about to be nameless.
The sky is a slice of lemon,
a hundred routes,
winging fellow travelers
to the same bitter core.

Below, houses sink
like squashed gnats
in the dust. Everyone strolls out
in bright scarves and petticoats
to greet me,
to congratulate me
on my questionable citizenship.
I deliberate
over the right sunglasses.

Just then a gang of banditos
picks me up
at the taxi station,
and leads me into the dark,
neon-lighted mesa.
The man at the desk, in front
of a white-washed tunnel,
hands out names
and thick, acrid drinks.

My mouth feels like a prickly pear.
Manicured succulents
are arranged in sun
at portholes in the dungeon halls.
The little green lizards
with malachite eyes are real,
but the mimosa tree petrifies.

I enter the decor,
of monumental, carved oak;
everything is attached
except the large mirror
and one plastic-sealed glass.
Even my suitcase doesn't belong to me.

Woman

Be a sapling
too supple to snap.
Thumb your nose as you
grow from your own spring.
Don't wait to churn up
secret twists of toxin
in your gnarled
knotholes.

Be a bee,
clean yellow buzz
of stripe and fur;
a sting!
Abort honey,
goo that sticks
in colorless puddles,
pap for infants.

In Season

Last summer, I smoothed
our path up the hill,
to the little house,
by the frail, lacy leaves
of the chrysanthemum
you were so careful not to trample,
when you filled the pails
at the pump.

I reveled in the wild grass,
barefoot and disheveled.
Before I knew,
I was a dough child, all yeast,
waiting to be kneaded.

We wore the season away
with your arms wed
to the narrow of my back.
You confided in Braille.
The brief sun fanned
the moss and trees;
green had no end,
until summer knelt,
with the fall,
of the first leaf.

One ripe red and yellow calyx
after another,
burst new buds,
and the chrysanthemum
bore two separate colors.

We boarded up the house,
left the path
blanketed with weeds.
Before the doorsill,
two brazen sentinels toss
side by side and tease.
Even snails wear their
shells all summer
in order to move on
to another season.

Perspective

The turnpike rolls back,
pulling the rug
out from under.
Each toll booth clock smirks
back the same hour.
I've worked off pounds
in this race until
chased to the last mile,
my lover's no more
than the faint twinge
of a stitch
on a neat, surgical incision.
I reach home free,
only to discover
I'm displaced.

III Separations

Birds of a Feather

Birds know how to fluff up
feather blankets, to blend. Monkeys
know how to touch, pick bugs
out of one another's hair. Seahorses couple,
cling, oscillate on end.

And we, supreme species,
charmed genus of oneness,
hermaphroditic sons hunch
petrified, deified,
at an impasse, armed.

Does the porcupine, or turtle,
the armadillo, sea urchin,
spiny echidna brace to sanctify
his onlyness, to exclude
his kind from his space?

We, alone, exquisite forms,
Are glorified by poets,
by clever artists who frame
our separateness in stone.

Testing I

I lay my hand between us, cautious.
I do not offer,
do not reach or make a pass,
merely place a gesture
suggestive under glass.

If you touch, you speak.
If you cover, you claim.
If you lift, you covet.
If you take, you restrain.
If you pull, you lust.

Touched hand gets
still hand. Covered hand
gets rigid hand. Lifted hand
gets withdrawn hand. Tugged hand
gets fist. Pulled hand gets slapped.

How much more clever if you
lay your hand still – yet near.
Now we are at an impasse.
How wonderful that we should
find the solution to our equalness.

Deaf Mute

The plants are dying again.
This time I'm determined
to concentrate. I read
all the directions, water carefully
with Vigaro and Hyponex.
The leaves droop, dry out,
brown slowly and drop.
Stems wither and hang.

It's a daily ritual, still
not enough. All the freshness,
and the green snuffs out as if it were
an account I've overdrawn –
too drained to renew.
I wait for the final
collapse. Don't tell me
to talk to plants.

Dance

Sometimes, I feel the closest I can
get to you is your underwear.
Something about the way
your socks smell
when I turn them right side out,
the shape of your drawers,
summons up exits, that make me
cram cigarettes and pour gin.

I search the shelves for something
to stuff in the empty pores
of what I have no more.
I shut the cupboard door.

I hate the addled mind
that showers and perfumes
in anticipation of your coming.
I could strip
in front of the t.v. screen,
but I can't stand here naked
and writhe – mute,
without cover.

You spill words
into the room
as you discard your clothes,
still dressed to kill.

Can't you even pluck me
like your guitar when I'm
so ready to sing?
Can't you cradle
my head in the nook
of your neck like your phone?
I'm softer and warmer and
willing to move where you go.

Stay away, let me dance
my solo – but no,
you see me standing free.
You dance your jiggeddy-jig,
rub my back and thighs,
pour those eyes down
into my bone and slide around
to bore out your hollow nest once more.

The Argument

Pins and needles
prick my skin.
Every limb is still.
A fleet of gnats
motors over the hills
to plant thistle.

At last another creature
inches aware. Your sword
is no longer a shield.
It jabs into my bed
of thorns.
You would not scare.

Portrait

Your picture is all over
the house in press clippings
and reviews. Still,
I can't remember
how you look. Just a glint
in the back of my head.
Alabaster chipped whitely
into ridges and dents,
coils like Medusa's,
nudges of nose holes,
a pair of glazed beads
without sockets, some
grinning slot, one side
higher than the other,
the arc of a headache,
now stares like a stuffed
fish on a platter,
iridescent. As I lean
forward to carve,
the mouth is a beak,
rapping like a woodpecker.

Separation at the corner of Santa Monica and La Cienega

At two a.m., you still at the studio,
push levers on the giant console.
I shift the wagon into first,
the flat back lined with limpid sacks
of children, pillows, covers borrowed
from the Hollywood Hawaiian Hotel.
Fueled on No-Doz, I pull into Rt.#5,
mid-Cal., six-lane highway, chute
through the night. One scant arc
of headlight pulls us up ahead.

At dawn, we climb gray-scrub
hills, sheep-dotted Salinas, scattered
phrases from Red Pony and Camino
Real. I search for a script,
the right pretext to awaken kids
to see this valley where will fought
wind in sunless dust – and lost.

On the first tail of traffic, we
coast into San Francisco. Behind a
Sunoco station, we dress; breakfast
at Alotti's on Fisherman's Wharf.
Proper tourists, we cable car from
Chinatown to Nob Hill, and down,
zigzag in low gear on Lombard,
the "crookedest street in the world,"
sip tea at the Japanese Garden
below the Golden Gate Bridge.

Do the "Historical Tour", San Francisco
Experience, The Fire Tower and Mission
of San Miguel. At dusk, we slice
srnog over the bridge into Sausalito.

We cart our picture post cards home
where you, still in the studio,
make your own history.

Home Movies

Your reel is a montage,
an over-dubbed, splice-free
35 millimeter, technicolor
fart. You stand astride the tracks,
face the speeding engine,
a giant, immovable object
meeting its counterpart.

Behind you, I make my own pictures
and cherish stills, black and white;
Rorschach silhouettes animated
by fingers of firelight
that slowly shift our shadows into flesh.

You stand in the spotlight
aroused by light and eyes.
Your voice leaps allegro,
your hands palm your thighs,
in sync with your sound track.

I, in the darkened niche
behind the projector,
lean and blink, try to focus,
to center on the screen.
The image is an old toy
train I maneuver
on the track of my dream.

Letter to Home

I'm taking jet trips,
moving so fast,
the clock struck morning
and ran on past.
The landscape in squares,
the highways in pairs,
are the same from the window,
from inclined chairs.
I stop at the Hertz desk,
back on the ground,
get a map to the gig
for the third time around;
take the airport exit,
turn left on Main,
could swear I just finished
doing the same.
Drop off my bag
at the Holiday Inn,
don't have to worry,
which city I'm in.
One phone call,
and I'm off on the job,
there's safety in numbers,
so bring on the mob.
Should I switch the pitch,
from the trip last week?
Would this group like it moody,
Or short and sweet?
Can't tell by the traffic,
or billboards or neon;
just another commission
I'm scheduled to be on.

Not 'til next morning,
at the airport again,
does some news hit my eye,
some local run-in,
that would have played there,
some input for patter,
but it's too late now,
and tomorrow won't matter.
Just as long as I'm flying,
my mind lost in the roar,
and no one comes with me,
who's heard it before,
I'll keep one step ahead
of that face in the crowd,
who can read through the grin,
that I'm crying out loud.

Nobility

I am devouring whole
lemons and boiled eggs,
fourteen of each, this
morning, and I'm not going
to quit just because
chewing is getting
to be uncomfortable.

The doctor says Vitamin C
and protein are good for me,
and, after all, they build
strong bodies. Just the same,
I wish you were here
to poke your fingers down my
throat and say, "Vomiting
also, is good when
you've had too much."

Narcissus

I am led by hand to the mat,
lie down between bodies, hesitate.
My mouth opens to see. Fingers
stroke cheek, kiss, neck
and mouth, breathe skin. I throb
familiar, raise
thighs, crook to receive,
blend rocking, press gender,
lock shuddering – bare.

A white bird hovers over. I
shield my ears. Too many
wings and tails. I shush my
host – ghost of remembered
past, roaming over these
intimate gestures of repetition,
whirr into memory
supple under my belly.
Lift me from this coupling!

The bird plummets onto water,
a storm borne leaf scissors
and sinks. I dive after,
thrashing through to land.

Dinner for Two

At dinner
I show my poems.
You say, "What class!"
I am all green,
splattering chatter
and lies, while
I offer my eyes
to your empty glass.

You pace the room
counter-clockwise. I try
to get next to you. The meal
is late and overdone.
I pretend to the kids
we are student and tutor.
You manage the distance,
a brake in my reel.

The room is a stage.
I spin out front,
cross the gulf.
You pull the curtain,
when you could
lift the trap door,
to let me
climb out of myself.

Poems are embraces,
but your engine is running.
The lights are on. You stand
and shift your feet.
I, dry ice, burn
black space, seek
some excuse to brush
your arm, touch your hand.

Tomorrow, I'll phone to see
who answers. I'd give a kiss
to see you smile. Now,
your motor roars in my ears.

Ambushed

By suspects and foreigners,
smiles slip, clocks slide off the mark,
although I, executioner, had set the
plan in motion. I did not, however,
invent the demonic barriers to play.
My quest is carried on passports
and plane tickets, and alerts officials,
all guardians of the garden across
darkness and beyond my goal.
The pilots keep regular schedules and
impeccable maintenance until I
arrive at the counter. Then they fly
over the departure zone Suddenly
codes are indecipherable. No computer
shows the hours and destination
on my travel instructions. The alphabet
is scrambled into alien acronyms
that fly on alternate days to mine. The
gates are closed; children, caught
in another time frame, don't wait.

In the end, an oversize T-shirt has
to cover all my tears and grime.
The night howls outside
my door and smudges dawn
with gray. It is either too early or
too late. Every other traveler
has a pass to get out. Finally, they
call my number. Perhaps it was worth
the trip, after all. Yet, on arrival,
there is no key to get in.

Comfort is masked
behind another language.
A scribbled message
alerts the clerk.
I am not about to be deported.
I try the number. Everyone is there.
The sun bursts out!
Who am I to blame?

IV Rituals

From Long Island to Bequia Bay

Alone in this room,
resolution sits
uncelebrated, within reach, yet
out of touch. I am in a rush
to check off this day exactly because
it is too significant, too soon.

Air burns generously at my soot-
gray bones, paints dusty rose
over virus and bile, curls and
thickens stringy hair
that starts my day
on the wrong foot.

We are cool and bright
at the end of a two-mile walk,
perched on the steep slant
of volcanic drop to a horseshoe
harbor sparsely dotted with huts
and sails of white.

We eat off the land;
fresh fish, banana, taro root,
plaintain, swim to a shipwreck and
dive to imaginary loot, slip
on the tracks to the reggae
beat of a native band.

Rangy, tousled groom,
you plant your square trunk
in the chair as a tree rooted to rock
resists the wind. There's no
transparency about you. You are
my mirror in this room.

No rescuers at all,
you hold me prisoner
in a mountain cage. Only goats
in the yard, a pig and hens,
brown, bare-bottomed chickens
or yellow-throats to heed my call.

We have come to kill
the past. Though there are fine
binoculars with the house, I don't
need them to see. Sunglasses remove
the glare, dim the distant blare
of another house on another hill.

You point your chin
like a hunter's nose at game.
You refuse to sleep, refuse to play,
refuse to fear, refuse to forget who
you are and push your pen through twenty
compulsive pages a day. You win.

A sign from above
should mark this night, painting
on mud, letting of blood, sticking
needles, branding scars, drinking
potions, burning, fasting, shrieking,
weeping, leching, love.

So we will return to losses anew
and gifts, and the same space
and waves, forgetting we saw time
sit still on a cedar rail.
Why is it I write
only about you?

Because of You

Pounding surf pours inside my
brain, spills me to the pillow. Too
soon, I face Bermuda sun. Light
in the porch corner of yesterday's tan
is a clock to signal afternoon.

The cycles are delivered and sit.
I will cook, write, sun, swim,
walk, sleep, type before riding.

But rented cycles can't be wasted.
We rev up; I lurch and buck. Too
much to contain; steering lever control,
drive to the left of the road.

We halt for directions — lever back,
jump in reverse. I miscalculate, zoom
to the edge of a drop, brake with my feet,
catch neutral, stop at the last second.

I detect a twitch of scorn. I must
prove to you when I need your
protection. So we run to Swizzle Inn,
a dart game and a beer with a one-
armed Black. I learn to keep score.

Stalactites and stalagmites elude
us in a limestone cave we can't
find. It's the wrong way home.
We turn. I forget to keep left,
weave to an oncoming car. Totally
jarred. I'm sure I can't go on.
But we started out for Spittle Pond.

My bare feet kiss ground. A grass
path cuts through pines, wood rot,
climbs sheer slopes of limestone
outcroppings, almost out of sight
of lava rock and surf. Close
to the summit we straddle a wind-curved
trunk. One step down, limey
crust gives, slipping me backward,
sliding fast, until I catch footing
in the gnarled roots. I need to rest.
Hidden from every side and above,
I curl into this secret sand nest under
bay grape cover. I exult in wind
and pounding surf sound, crab
holes and ant hills, surrounded
by you. A branch brushes my forehead,
five leaves, and safe in the center,
a new sprig stretches to wavering sky.

It's so far to home. But suddenly,
I know. You will not let me die.

Detoxification

We return without a word,
you to your typewriter, I to my book,
pledged to a pact, unspoken, unheard,
after dining. I pause to look
at your composure, slip behind
you and reach out lightly
to stroke the back of your neck,
find the tendon beside your ear.
You pose, palms midair, amidst thoughts,
raise your head, half turn, swivel
slowly round to press
the comma in my eyes,
for me to finish the phrase.
Gently as gossamer you caress
your check across mine.
I meet you and hold still
the tentative test
of your lips. You fold
away the top of my dress
murmuring against my breast,
coax my hands down over your chest,
furling into a curve,
about warm air. We rest
drawing it in. You rise evenly,
to match breath and nerve.
We clasp, reading eyes,
reading touch of skin,
reading lips. How easily we align.
We pair, without dark, without talk,
without grass, without wine.

Rain

You're obsessed with rain
especially night-music;
the harder the better,
the louder the wetter,
sloshing down gutters, splashing
at windowpanes, drumbeats
chant numbness –
pounding you soundless.

Rain, pouring
its amniotic sack,
watery reassurance,
a libertarian lullaby;
release and refrain.
Release you can't allow,
except in the dark,
through torrents of rain.

As storm clouds,
pushed to bursting,
mourn for a field
thirsting to green,
you preen your roundness
in cumulus swells
and gush tears around
and down and down.

Off Shore

I

I sing old love songs,
lies, amidst invisible gnats,
in a limestone
cave. You pace, singing,
too, for the time to come
when the mood will turn
on a word or two. The space
outside is a stretch
of ground shell cliffs
etched on the sea, hedging
palm and pine. What's
shutting us in is my own
chill against the light,
circling and scratching
on the sand, whining
in this low cell.

II

I am purified, anointed,
free of tossing down vodka
and juice, chain smoking,
I have found a spot
where my stomach
sits, a bulb silently
sipping mud and air,
sucking me into its bud.

III

This is a restoration by fire;
we gather dead wood under
the oleander hedges, petrified
roots trapped in the creviced
tunnels of limestone ledges.

You read *Esquire*,
page by page,
rip off and crumple paper
to toss in the fire,
a movie review of *Going Places*,
the French film
Emmanuelle,
*The Private Life of J. Edgar
Hoover*, *Singing in
The Reign of Beverly Sills*.

I plot a ritual of medicines,
dried leaves of the bay.
I lay the fire and chant their names:
monkeypod, bay grape, burrs of the spiny
spruce, parched juniper sprigs,
curled fronds of Bermuda palm.
The cottage basket is filled
with layers, properly
cured, a magic spell to feed our
new life waiting for flames.

Storm Warning

A tempest throws a siege
on the town, breaks up
the neighbors, blasts

an octopus into the room
where she cuts patterns
she can't control. The storm

door slams back and shatters
glass clear across the gutter,
breaks its hinges and ruptures.

Some of the pattern pieces
lie in piles. Still,
she has no sewing machine.

Darkness fondles him,
dusk turns on spotlights
in a room full of scraps.

Restless arms are wriggling
in her head — out of water.
The bathtub is a dirty

clothes bin. At least the hearth
is quiet. He says, "Come sit on
the warm cushions."
She brings her pins.

Contract

In a new coat,
not for the company
president, but as rabbits thicken
their fur before snow,
and squirrels their subterfuge,
I meet the house,
and the host,
who has you on tape.

What begins here
after the contract is signed,
after Thanksgiving,
is older than this house,
older than we,
and not grateful.

You go in ahead,
to the studio.
I am left with the bag.

Precisely at six,
all the lights are doused.
One after another,
matching noses of candlelight
from wall niches, rafters
and balcony, fuse studio
tape and reefer fumes,
appropriate the air and render
me invisible.

A long log
with even blue flames
turns without blackening
and does not burn.
I want to change clothes.
I am constrained
for this meeting.

You disappear.
I chain smoke,
scribble a thread of lyric
on a match cover.

Later, alone
in the dark bed,
I suppress a smoldering cry,
"Thief!"

Equinox

It happens every Fall. Mounting
the Equinox. The day has no equator
to divide your meteorological
excesses. Some cause moves you.
Last year politics, now a record
contract; demon clock
in you that storms through
perpetual nights. You are a giant
moth, beating triple time
for yesterday's idle talk, outside
my window, though the door is open
and the light is on.

At the winter solstice, the moth
spins a tight cocoon and crawls
in to hibernate. A brief season
in the last recess of me,
until Spring melts the old
memories that push you out.
The chrysalis births a hairy bear,
prancing from the cave to celebrate
renewal in round dances.
Rejoice midsummer grisly
knave, and reprobate.
I can't catch you this late.

V Beginning at the Dead End

First Step

Wishing for the definition
of whole apple in its skin,
cheese in its rind,
I am unwilling
to be sliced open.

The tender fruit curls inside,
flesh needs to press
out of bounds, tentacles
explore the space between
raw nerves and encounters.

There's a promise there.
These antennae skirt and slip
around abandonment,
stretch, just short of breaking,
Looking for kin.

Rescue

I run from the Maui cottage,
too small for our mushrooming fears;
run from broken windows and blades,
the comfort of a fifth of rum,
into the shallows, under bullets
of rain to the dark freedom of Molotoi.
Pocked and razorbacked lava lays out
spiked stones too sharp to step on,
too close to stride over black sand.
I must last long enough, fast
enough to swim; to reach the stretch
of sea between Molotoi and me.

You take me, force me to a
ground of needles and dead leaves.
Crystal nails bore straight into skin;
pack me on the lava back.
You will not trust me to wait,
pull me back to the hut, grab
blankets from shelves and beds,
race us back to spread a dry
ground of bedding on the damp,
spread a layer of you full and hard,
pull me under your ribs,
put your back to the nails.

I cower under the lost battle.
There is no triumph. Only alms.
Yet something new was there from that day
if I had listened to your grateful humming,
soothing a safe tune with the rain,
and the waves and the wailing palms.

Parallels

"Two people who love the dream above
all else would soon vanish altogether.
One of them must be on earth to hold
The other down."
                    —Anäis Nin, *Under the Glass Bell*

I fantasize perfect symmetry;
couples in dead heat,
swimmers paired from gunshot
to finish line. Two skiers
schuss the parallel run.
Tennis partners match set,
runners break the ribbon as one.
Pas de deux, unison, duet.

You and I, the odd couple, mismatch,
as athletes, performers, playmates.
But how we fit as twin architects
of dreams! Together we create
cities of the can-be-done. You
break unmarked trails. I draw plans
for debate with hinges and moveable
parts that interlock. You bridge spans
between wish and possibility. I smooth
edges, push, finish, negotiate residue
and schism; all immediate thrust and dare.

You build the avid, vital rhythm.
Ah, what a dream when
we can also sculpture
inner space. When thought
and sight connect to stop
escape. To chart the new,

no scheme so great
as to see tenderly,
straight into me, into you.

Tapestry

Your cloth comes from history,
carved in a statue in 1690,
in Springfield, Massachusetts,
heir to a grand longevity.
Your clothes tarnish with time,
and the threads of clairvoyance.

Your woof thrusts into many-splendered
chaos of impulse, risk, conflict;
the unexpected and improvised.
Your warp competes, reaches
on tiptoes, dancing
promises unafraid.

Your full vocabulary covers
all the languages of texture;
nubs, knots, thick wool, homespun,
and original open weave.
Uneven edges
in endless soliloquy.

Here is a tapestry of colossal belief,
of gaping wonder and eloquence,
I am confident the shuttle will never
cease. The carpet will increase;
a farsighted and fertile
canvas for search and zeal.

Vibration

There's a fine line between us
stringing real pearls
that can't be replaced
because they were gathered by divers
at the shores of Nayerit.
You keep pulling,
trying to snap it,
to split the wire,
to break through,
yet, I have woven that wire
of viscera and bone you don't know
not hip or pelvis or vertebrae
that fracture and split.

You stab sword and knife,
spin backward.
You see me snore
and smile,
steal in the dark, lift
the wire to pass under.
Don't you know I never sleep any more?

I wiggle fabulous fingers and sing
abracadabra and alakazam
over it to strain taut
a fiber that strays
and stretches out of reach
when you kick blind
ass hoofs sideways.

Will you go mad,
beat your brains blue,

see only mortar and brick,
then bashed and bruised
retreat into mud prints?

I wish to take your callused finger,
chew the dead head off,
bite bone,
bleed muscle and artery,
bleed watery waste,
bleed all hot blue
stuff pumping through
your tri-chambered chicken heart,

spill the stench over my bare feet,
lick at my ankles,
slosh up calves and thighs,
invade my torso,
suck my arms into whirlpools,
break against my breast,
a torrent pouring into my mouth and ears.

I can spit it all out!

and rise on tip toes,
turn you around,
run your finger now soft
with new skin
on this filament
of opalescent tears.

Do you feel the vibration?

Stripping In

We meet again. You goggled
and masked, I gagged
and flannelled. We stick
brick to brick, build
bunkers, barbed wire
barriers. Keep out!
No trespassing! You spew
torrents of phrases
from inside a coat of mail.

Ivy-covered thorns trap
passing briefcases
full of calendars,
appointment books,
plane tickets in coats,
jackets, jeans, sweat
shirts, sweaters. Clasp
pins, closings – closer.
Helmets and goggles.

I swell and puff,
a reptile too fat
to shed. The padding
hardens to scales of iron.
Our armor clanks
loudly in the night.

A deafening clamor shakes
the small room, accumulates
weight, presses against
tongues and breasts,
strangling attempts
to cry for help. Lungs
are about to collapse
until you throw
off your metal.

Then, struck, you reach
out to break mine.
We are too naked
to run, too exposed
to stand free
and shiver. We stretch
to soothe depressions
from hard steel, mesh
open in the dark.

Imagine Moments of Soft Wonder

I

Imagine winds of ripe wonder,
hovering desires immediately more lawful
than breezy thieves who nightly, slide under
doors. Summon confident gusts, awful,
to blow away offices, planes, concert halls.
Splinter shutters without so much as a tap
on the wood, melt windowed walls
of ice, pass through fiberglass curtains and chart
the room this side of the windowsill.

Seawinds shift on shafts of air,
surprise the room's own currents and still
their lecturing. Fingers of swells sprint
over knuckles, lift hands from piles
of contracts and blueprints,
break the incessant cycles of dials.
They run the ink, blot the numbers and lists
of secret categories and fugitive plans. Toss
out fault, breathe at brow and breast a final twist
into intimate furrows to dilute salt and loss.

II

In the evening the snow comes,
patterns on the artificial light to blur
edges of furnishings and the aim
of management, to stutter and slur
over instructions. The kaleidoscopic show
swirled midair; a perpetual spew.
The only impulse to flight was in the snow.
But it was too soft and new

to melt knobs and controls. We stepped back
from the impending avalanche. There must be a lull soon
in the steady onslaught. We would rain the slack
back in line. Make the snow play our tune.
It is important to cherish dissonances to keep face.
We draw all our skin in knife edged
silhouettes on white space.
Now it is a matter of life
or death. Flushed at the threatening chain
of events, every nerve end taut, we poise
wary, willing to wait out the blizzard and strain
for a break to move on to safety and noise.

III

Then the precipitation rains and falls
on the air, breathless at first;
we, numb under the lapping at our shell,
see spasms of heat lightening burst
into the room, illuminate and pour
over brown boundaries. Then, green
with algae, the rain wipes sore
brows and fingers to iridescent clean.
Simultaneously, we work the pumps and tread
water. All the time losing ground.
All this water puts us in dread
of the flood. It was alright to surround
the desert, needful of our dry places. It began to teem
into deep undercurrents destined to rout
memory, destined to search out dreams.
Finally, motives are a washout!
We plunge into deeper breathing offshore,
The floodgates are open too late to stall
torrents purging every pore.
We can't help but take the free fall.

Circle

She thought she would die before him.
He thought he would sing
'til one hundred.
No Exit. A ring
around her need for reverie,
a need to nourish his light,
both real and potential. She would glow
in his shadows and throw back bright
reflections. They began
in a heat of the first degree,
rising toward promises,
prospects toward grand symmetry.

She believed she might die for him.
Nothing that happened before
he came was of any import.
He was the complete core
of her center, both seed and fruit.
He was the future. There was a sense
of safety in accepting
the band, his circumference.
If the ring broke and the stuff
in the middle broke the border,
fell end over end,
life was simply outside meaning or order.

Suppose she should live for him?
At once she could try to take his place,
large and luminous; a legend,
father, performer, architect of dreams and spaces.
Or since he has run with the wind,
she could gather what he has sown,
cast the seed to the sun,
step from the shadows, own
love better by living, keep
the circle turning, thrive
on curiosity, spend the rest of life learning
to circle towards the vital, alive.

A poet, writer, teacher and advocate, Sandy Chapin is the mother of five children and grandmother of seven. Her late husband, Harry Chapin, had his only #1 hit, "Cats in the Cradle", with lyrics taken from one of Sandy's poems. The song entered the Grammy Award Hall of Fame in 2010. Sandy is chair of the board of The Harry Chapin Foundation in Huntington, NY, and serves as chairperson of Long Island Cares/The Harry Chapin Food Bank.

Entries is Sandy's first published book of poetry.

Made in the USA
Charleston, SC
19 July 2016